# For Ella and Bella

Oxfam would like to acknowledge, with thanks, the following photographers:
Annie Bungeroth (pages 6–7), Marj Clayton (pages 22–23), Howard Davies (pages 5 and 26–27),
Sarah Errington (pages 12–13 and cover), Jim Holmes (pages 10–11), Ley Honor Roberts (pages 14–15),
Crispin Hughes (pages 18–19 and 24–25), Philippe Lissac (pages 16–17)
Rajendra Shaw (pages 20–21 and back cover) and Sean Sprague (pages 8–9).
The book begins on page 6.

First published in Great Britain in 2006 by
Frances Lincoln Children's Books, 4 Torriano Mews,
Torriano Avenue, London NW5 2RZ

www.franceslincoln.com

British Library Cataloguing in Publication Data available on request

ISBN 1-84507-330-4

Printed in China

1 3 5 7 9 8 6 4 2

Oxfam GB will receive a 5% royalty for each copy of this book sold in the UK.

# Hair

## Kate Petty

**FRANCES LINCOLN CHILDREN'S BOOKS**
in association with

 **Oxfam**

It is cold in the high mountains of Pakistan. Pedan and Samullah have thick hair that is cut short so it doesn't get in their eyes.

My hat keeps my head warm.

Ana is combing Maria's hair outside their home in Guatemala. She is going to tie it back with a red scrunchie.

I want to look like my big sister.

Linh lives in Vietnam.
He is washing his hair at
the well outside his house
before he goes to school.

It's hard washing just my hair.

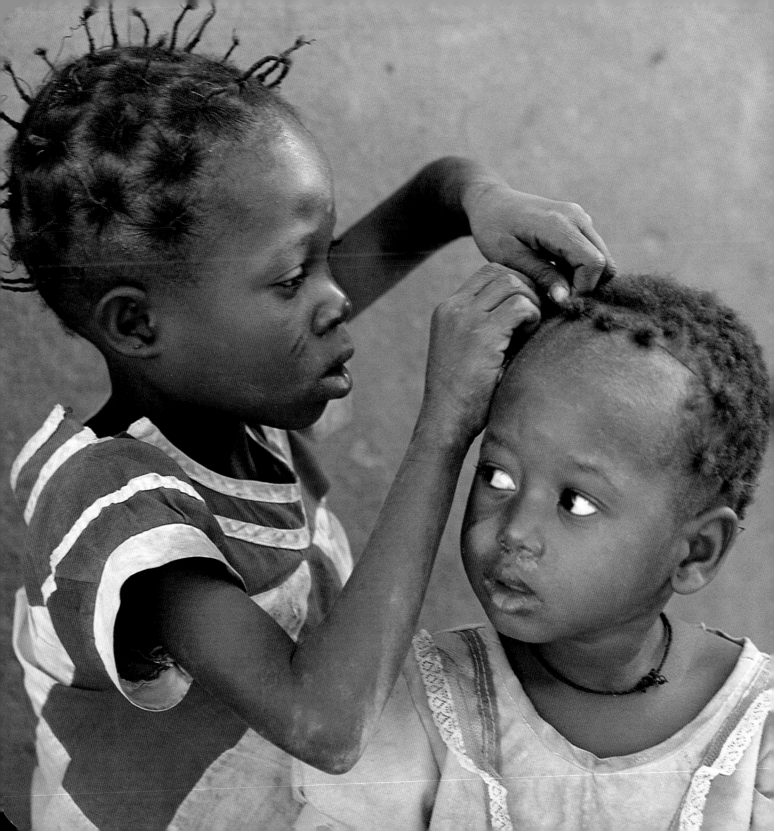

Felicia and Anongee are friends.
They live in Ghana. Felicia parts
Anongee's curls into neat rows.
Then she ties them into
little clumps.

I have to sit
very still.

Martha likes to make her baby sister Ruby look pretty. She has picked some flowers from outside their house in the United States of America.

This pink flower is my favourite.

Doesn't Catherine look lovely with these beads in her plaits? She lives in a small African country called Togo.

My beads feel nice when I shake my head.

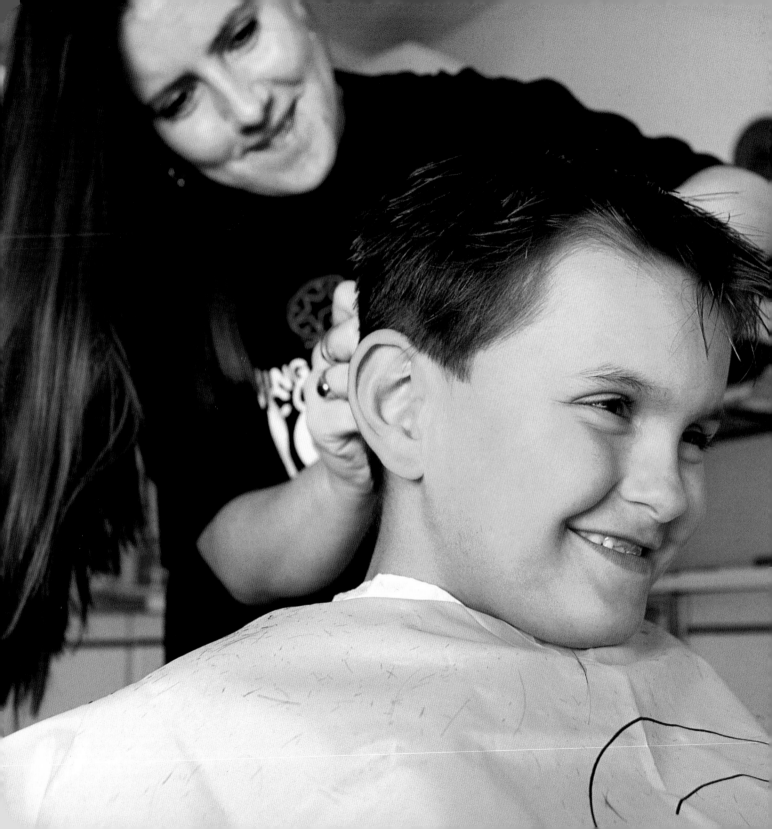

Nathaneal is having a haircut at his home in the United Kingdom. He uses gel to make it stand up.

I like my hair to look cool.

Shakeel lives in India. He wants to look smart for the festival today. He rubs oil into his hair to keep it in shape. The oil is scented with spices.

My hair oil smells nice in the hot sun.

Liliana must have the longest plaits in the world! She lives in the highest city in the world, too – La Paz in Bolivia.

I tie my plaits back when I am at work.

Wolo's friends have done her hair. In Burkina Faso where she lives, some of the styles have names like 'Sevens' or 'Alpha' or 'Scales'.

My spiky hair stays up with wire!

Kim lives in a village in Cambodia called Prek Chdoar. She has long hair, which she likes to wear loose.

I can tie my hair back if it gets too hot.

United States

United Kingdom

Guatemala

Burkina Faso

Ghana

Togo

Bolivia

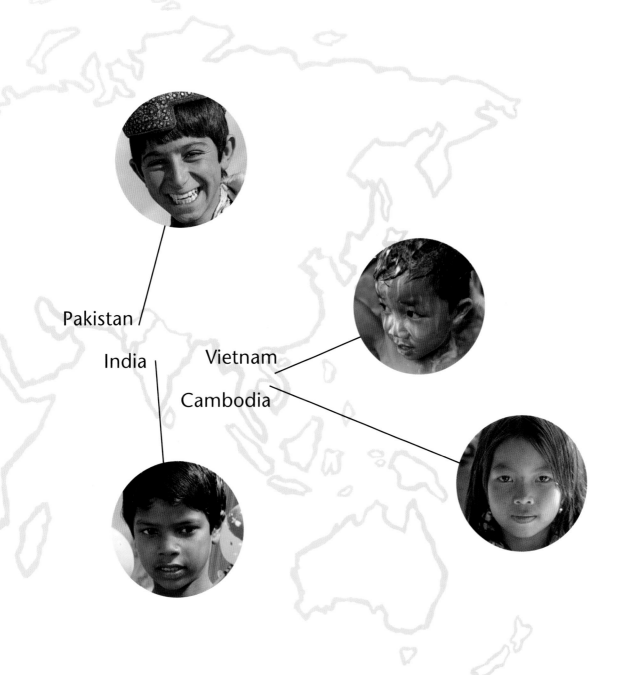

Pakistan

India

Vietnam

Cambodia